Hope, R

Hope, Respect and Trust

Valuing These Three

Joel Edwards

Authentic

10 09 08 07 06 05 04   7 6 5 4 3 2 1

First published in 2004 by Authentic Media
9 Holdom Avenue, Bletchley, Milton Keynes, Bucks., MK1 1QR, UK
and Box 1047, Waynesboro, GA 30830-2047, USA
www.authenticmedia.co.uk

British Library Cataloguing in Publication Data

A catalogue record for this book is available from the British
Library

ISBN 1-85078-589-9

Cover design by 4-9-0 ltd
Print Management by Adare Carwin
Printed and bound by AIT Nørhaven A/S, Denmark

Contents

Acknowledgements

Nothing worth doing is ever accomplished on your own. I am indebted therefore to those who have helped me in this enterprise. Much thanks goes to John Smith, Malcolm Duncan and other members of the Evangelical Alliance staff for their invaluable help. Special thanks is also due to friends such as Roger Smith, Laurence Singlehurst, Matt Summerfield and Patrick Dixon who have been great encouragers in developing Values as a missions discourse. Thanks, too, to Julia Murphy who cast a keen eye on the text. And a very special thanks to my PA, Vikki McLachlan, who rescued me more than once to meet seemingly impossible deadlines.

This book has been a modest attempt to articulate a new idea in missions. Because it is the product of developing thoughts it is likely to have some obvious gaps. But it is offered as a small contribution to the great task of missions.

Foreword

Imagine being on an ocean liner, crashing through heavy seas, and discovering that there is no one on the bridge. You learn that the captain has been locked below with all of his charts and compass. The ship is completely unguided.

At first we might be glad to see the back of the captain. From a distance we had spotted him strutting around the deck, clad in ancient regalia, giving the impression that he was piloting a nineteenth-century sailing ship rather than a modern deluxe cruiser.

But then we realise: we are on a vessel powering across the seas with no sense of direction, no one at the wheel and no one to guide us. There may be icebergs out there!

So what shall we do? Let the old fellow out so he can parade around the bridge shouting 'shiver me timbers'? Probably not. We would be better advised to tiptoe into his cabin while he is still sleeping, gently remove his compass and charts and call the passengers together to plot a course and steer the ship safely to it.

We live today in the twenty-first century with no clear set of values to guide us. There is nobody on the bridge and we have no idea where we are going. The values framework, based on our Judaeo-Christian heritage has been eroded these past fifty years as we the church have allowed ourselves to get bogged down in irrelevant issues. Society, greatly in need of the truths and values that flow from our faith, ploughs on regardless, heading for an uncertain destination.

So we need to launch ourselves upon a new conversation with those around us to spark a fresh understanding about the values that must underpin and shape our culture. The work done by Joel Edwards and his team at the Evangelical Alliance in recent years is an important attempt to engage society in a new conversation about things that really matter: who are we, what do we believe, and how should we live?

This book neatly summarises the key themes of that discourse and challenges all of us to take part in it. The specific virtues of hope, trust and respect are well chosen and resonate with the needs of this age – largely because there is an absence of hope: trust lies in tatters at our feet and respect is a stranger to many.

This is a conversation that must well up from within a compassionate, non-judgemental church, and spill over into our streets and into the public square. Whether in responding to international terrorism or sweeping globalisation; whether in helping us to improve inner city education or wrestle with the scourge of drugs; whether in shaping our approach to genetic engineering or bio-ethics, these values must guide us.

I commend Joel for grappling with this challenge in such a vibrant and thought-provoking way. There may well be icebergs and hidden rocks ahead, but we are better placed to avoid them if the people on the bridge have been handed back their charts and compass.

Gary Streeter, MP

Introduction: A Question of Values

How it all began

In 1998 a group of 15 leaders met to discuss a new way of doing missions. The original plan was to use the Ten Commandments to promote a mission about the values by which we live and make our moral choices. Not everyone was convinced, but we were left with a desire to say something together which would engage our culture in a different way.

Not all of the 15 Christian leaders were convinced by the notion of values. Some suggested that the popular rhetoric would have died by 2002. Others felt that values were rather elusive: anything based on the Ten Commandments would prove anachronistic.

Quite frankly it was a challenging task with many important lessons along the way. What emerged was *Facevalues* – a holistic response to current questions of our day. The mission was spread over a six-month period, culminating in November 2003. Each month different themes were identified and churches were encouraged to pick up the themes in their local context. The themes included: Where Society is Heading, Trust,

Love, Respect and Our Children's Future. The final and major focus was on Forgiveness, and included a church's 'Say Sorry Sunday' and a National Forgiveness Day.

The mission was both exciting and exasperating. I was quite prepared to reflect on the experience indefinitely! But there was no doubt about it: society still seemed to be struggling to recover values by which to live in the absence of absolute ideals.

As I chatted with friends and reflected on the positive things we had learned, it became evident that Values as a mission discourse still offered Christian witness; what a colleague Mike Parker described as an example of 'wisdom evangelism'. We decided to return to the mission identifying three themes with which to develop our conversation with our culture: Hope, Trust and Respect.

Why Values?

Today, post-Christendom Britain has become more like a man with a tattoo declaring, 'I love Jane'. The only problem is that Jane left him 25 years earlier and he just has no idea what to do with the tattoo. And we have a lot of evidence that this is the case. In 1996 Gallup showed that out of 1151 adults 35 per cent knew what Gethsemane was; 40 per cent had no idea what Good Friday was about. In a culture that has lost the grammar of Christian faith, we need to tap into the urgent conversation of the culture.

But if we have lost common Christian grammar, we may still be able to learn universal sign language. The values by which we live and determine our quality of life may yet offer us a way back into the conversation.

There is no truth in the rumour that society doesn't want to hear from the church. In times of national or local disasters it is clear that people turn to the church for consolation and guidance. When the BBC's *Soul of Britain* survey was published in 2000, 82 per cent wanted the church to speak out against poverty, 75 per cent said we should condemn racism and 70 per cent still wanted to hear our voice on global inequalities.

Our modern world puts a high price on the existence of personal freedoms. Chief Rabbi Dr Jonathan Sacks reminds us that the very concept of liberty cannot be separated from questions of values. And as the American writer and activist Jim Wallis helpfully points out, values are at the very heart of our political and cultural issues. 'The language of values is particularly appropriate to an individualistic society,' says Christian ethicist David Attwood, and particularly so because it is the language of economics which drives Western society. 'It gives a way of discussing moral points of view with widely different rationales.'[1]

Values give us a way into the cacophony of moral debates about what it means to be alive in the twenty-first century. For many unchurched people, values may be the password to their private realities. And it will also be a key to our authentic involvement in public policy. Both Wilberforce and Martin Luther King fought public policy on the value of human dignity and what it meant to be made in God's image. Another Christian ethicist David Cook is correct in saying, 'values are a key aspect of our survival both as a society and as individual members of that society.'[2] Mark Greene's contribution to *Christianity & Renewal* (June 2004) makes the point very helpfully. 'The Challenge of the twenty-first century church is not one that can be addressed by a new set of programmes...The core issue is not programmes but ethos, not activities but values.' How can we possibly be excluded from such a conversation?

The idea of discourse will not appeal to everyone. Some will see it as an unhelpful distraction from the task of preaching or evangelism. We need to be clear: Christian faith instils the confidence that lives and communities can be changed through the power of forgiveness that is received through the life, death and resurrection of Jesus. T. S. Eliot's *Idea of a Christian Society* included the reminder that Christianity involves more than good moral arguments: it believes in truth. But mission-discourse should not be undervalued. The way to personal and community transformation may start with a common interest in a drink of water between two people at a well (John 4).

In a theological symposium on a *Movement For Change*, June 2002, Anna Robbins warned against the 'culture war' approach to Christian witness in favour of 'study dialogue'. The latter, she suggests, 'approaches ethics with a certain humility'.[3] In today's post 9/11 environment Moltmann's advice against fundamentalism is sobering. 'A faith which makes itself impregnable to attack is no longer in a position to attack . . . Its safe stronghold becomes its prison.'[4]

In a world where the press so often sets the pace, Christians face the danger of our complicated in-house conversations ending up like an irrelevant slanging match on the pavement. Perhaps even worse, we may sound like someone 'out of sync' – barging into a discussion about nuclear physics to ask if people like bananas! If there is evidence that people in our culture are looking for values by which to live, or are *confused* by the absence of values they once had, then there should surely be room for Christians to get involved in those conversations. At the dawn of the third millennium it is clear that politicians and the public are looking around for help as they discuss important ideas such as *responsibility, tolerance, diversity, community* and *security*. The overall impression is that the church is either ill-equipped or uninterested in what people are talking about.

Far from side-stepping preaching and evangelism, a mission-discourse about values may empower many Christians to become involved in the conversation – going beyond their inhibitions about evangelism to conversational Christian witness. It's learning sign language.

Values and virtues

But values need a health warning. In a 1997 address to an Evangelist Conference, Lesslie Newbigin warned that values could be a concession to pluralism. It is a serious caution and, as David Attwood has also advised, values are all too easily confused with morality.

In the same vein, Dr Jonathan Sacks' critical book *The Politics of Hope*, has expressed concerns about replacing the classic term 'virtues' (socially prized dispositions) by the more modern and quite different word 'values' (individually selected preferences).[5] Drawing from Alisdair MacIntyre's *After Virtue*, Dr Sacks argues that the Enlightenment has basically distorted our common language of morality, fragmenting conversations about morality. Sacks' work has demonstrated very clearly just how far Western society has drifted away from our Judaeo-Christian virtues.

Christian certainties are no longer the undisputed templates of our cultural norms. Its institutions may still be the official caretakers of what is right but can no longer claim exclusive rights to the title deeds. Today, everything from our chat-show morality to the

complicated politics of our bio-ethical debates under-
lines the fact that freedom and morality recognise no
obligation to Christian faith.

Christian convictions don't begin with values. They
are drawn from the great virtues of the Holy Spirit who
shapes our character (Gal. 5:22–25) and worldview
(2 Cor. 5:17). Christian virtue must therefore typify the
Christian communities who have come into a new relationship with Jesus Christ and life in the Spirit.

But this is not the point from which our society starts.
In the rejection of revelation and the growing erosion of
absolutes, people talk about values. Values dictate the
conversation of a culture that has begun a dialogue
without any obligations to God.

In the same way that Jesus asked for water and ended
up talking about eternal life, we talk about values in
order that we might talk about virtue.

What this book aims to do

Any discussion about values has to be rooted in important themes. But in identifying key themes we are
equally in danger of short-term thinking. This book aims
to lay a rationale for approaching values as a pre-
evangelistic route into the mindset of our culture. But
equally as a means by which we join in the prevailing
conversations of our day in order that we might bring
biblical perspectives to the debate.

Faith, hope and love are cardinal virtues of Christian
teaching. But they also resonate with people beyond the
life of the Christian church. Who in our society can live
without them? What is clear is that the language of faith,
hope and love has also been recast into a contemporary
vocabulary. I want to suggest that these are trust,

diminished hope and respect. These values for which our world seeks are but contemporary mirror images of the great virtues of faith, hope and love. A conversation about values could well lead to firm commitments of these virtues.

My purpose here is to enable the church to develop a more pro-community posture. People think of Christians as being *against* things. Over the past two decades the church has become synonymous with heated debates about women's ordination, homosexuality and a decline in attendance. Perhaps our dialogue about values will give us opportunities to say something new to a culture that seldom equates our voice with *good news*. As we engage in conversations about the well-being of our culture it may register the fact that we are *for* better communities. And in our journey with values we have already seen its capacity to engage with our communities in meaningful ways.

For example, during the Evangelical Alliance's focus on forgiveness, a West London school downloaded our materials on forgiveness to use in their school assemblies. And over the Christmas and New Year 2003/4 a local congregation dropped three separate advertisements through my front door inviting me to hear discussions on hot issues affecting the local community. Each was an invitation to attend a meeting in the community about hope.

An ongoing dialogue about values at a local and national level will be a part of the drip-feeding of hope in our world. It will be an important contribution to what William Wilberforce described as a 'reformation of manners'. If people hear us speaking about judgement, they must also hear us working for better values.

One

Faith – the Ability to Trust

Let your Yes be Yes.   (Mt. 5:37)

I think that deception is the real enemy of trust.
                                                    (Onora O'Neil)

'Trust me, I'm a doctor' – a phrase so often the punch-line for jokes, mostly with some kind of innuendo attached to it. But behind its frivolous use is the reality that most of us do trust doctors. In the aftermath of cases such as that of Harold Shipman, we are still willing to tell them intimate things about ourselves, for them to see us at our worst, even to touch us in ways that would be a criminal offence if anyone else did so. What this also tells us is that sadly, 'trust me' needs qualification. Why should I trust you? – because, 'I'm a doctor'. Replace that with 'Trust me I'm a politician' (double-glazing salesman, estate agent, taxman – a Christian?) and we soon begin to realise that we don't easily give our trust to people. Who is asking for our trust determines whether we choose to trust them or not. Of course that doesn't mean that trust isn't a core value on which we build personal and corporate relationships. But there are plenty of people who feel, more than ever, that there is a famine of trust in our society.

Admittedly there has never been a Utopian age when trust was universally present. But in recent years its decline has become the hallmark of modern insecurities. A casual glance at the mentions of 'trust' in our national newspapers indicates the degree to which trust as a topic for debate has moved to the centre of our collective consciousness. One broadsheet journalist admitted that his paper mentions 'trust' around seventeen times every day, compared with a mere six times a week only five years ago. Indeed, in the last few months I have personally collected a file full of articles on the subject with relative ease. But it's an easy task to provide desperate headlines and examples of where trust has gone missing in areas such as business, public life and institutions, the Church and in human relationships. The more demanding task will be to work out just why trust appears to be diminishing and what we should do about it.

A biblical look at trust – faith

From the very beginning, God himself acted in trust when he made the world and set Adam and Eve within it. In calling them to subdue and steward the earth, he delegated to them responsibilities which he might very well have exercised himself. Even today, as the world faces a whole range of ecological challenges from global warming to deforestation, God entrusts us with working together to find solutions. In commanding man and woman to become one flesh, to be fruitful and multiply, and to name the animals, God devolved some of his own creative power and took the risk that such power might be wielded wrongly (Gen. 12:6–2:24). When this did happen, he did not abandon his errant children, but drew them back to himself. He sustained the institution of marriage as one of the most important arenas of trust between humans, and between humankind and himself. And crucially he also forged covenants with Noah, Abraham, Moses and David – solemn contracts which affirmed the relational nature of trust, but which emphasised that trust also depends on recognising objective laws which compel us to honour and respect others, for the good of the whole community.

In Scripture, we see plenty of people 'entrusted' with responsibilities, and plenty who betray trust. In both the Old and New Testaments, the concept of 'trusting' someone is often interchangeable with the idea of 'having faith' in them. So the Israelites are described in Exodus 14:31 as 'trusting' or 'having faith' in Moses. Although their trust is largely justified, Moses fails to enter the Promised Land because he exceeds his authority in a way that risks undermining that trust (Ex. 18:24–26; Num. 20:10–13). In 1 Chronicles 9:22, 21:2, men are appointed by David and Samuel to guard the tent of meeting and the ark within it, and are described as thus occupying an 'office of trust'. Lest the seriousness of their task be underestimated, one need only recall the fate of Uzzah, who subsequently forgot the trust placed in him and touched the ark, dying instantly as a result (1 Chr. 13:10). David himself succeeded a king, Saul, who tragically betrayed the trust placed in him, and who foreshadowed the betrayals of many kings afterwards – from Jeroboam's idolatry, through Ahab's corruption, to Ahaz's doomed alliance with Assyria. In the gospels, Jesus entrusted the Twelve with a mission of evangelism, healing and deliverance, but it's not long before Judas betrays his Master's life and before Peter denies that he ever knew him (Mt. 10:1–15; 26:14–16; 26:69–75).

Ultimately these episodes are not simply about the trust of one person or group for another: they are about trusting in God, and being trusted by God. Moses compromised an authority, which God had granted, and it is God who barred him from Canaan. It was not the tent of meeting or the ark themselves which needed trusting, so much as the God whose presence dwelt within them. Israel's kings might periodically have let their people down, but in doing so, they let God down even more. On one level, Peter and Judas' betrayals of trust are very human acts of weakness; but they are each associated with the devil because they are seen more profoundly to betray God himself (Mk. 8:33; Jn. 13:2). The psalmist may be using hyperbole when he cries, 'Do not put trust in princes, in mortals, in whom there isn't any help', but the point is clear in the final analysis: our trust must be in God rather than humanity (Ps. 146:3).

As ever, Jesus is our paradigm, our model for living who speaks of what it means to be fully human. Nowhere else is trust in God and in others more exemplified than in his life, death and resurrection. As a baby, God entrusted Jesus to the care of Mary and Joseph as his parents, but also to the whole community. Has there ever been a more trusting and life-affirming act than God handing over his only Son to a world full of sin? As Jesus himself reached adulthood, he continued to 'entrust' himself to others – submitting to baptism by John, washing his disciples' feet and, eventually, giving himself up to the authorities so that he might die for the sins of the world – humbly handing himself over to God in obedience, to us in service and to both in sacrificial love.

God calls us to trust – just as Jesus was called to trust. But he also trusts us again and again. We learn to trust God as he trusts us – without this we do not have the kind of mutuality at the heart of all things – a Trinitarian God. We know the Bible is concerned about trust because through the actions of a Triune God, it is woven into the fabric of the creative order and society's well-being. Trust is an attribute of God and it is a gift of God to his creatures. Trust, therefore, becomes one of the most basic ingredients in human relationships. To trust is to become a person.

From a Christian point of view, faith in a trust-worthy God gives the perfect relationship from which to practise the precarious art of trusting relationships. Its eternal perspective and final accountability keeps a steady course between legitimate scepticism and suffocating cynicism.

Trust is the mirror image of faith. And like faith it's the substance of interaction between two conscious entities. Faith alone is useless: it has no meaning as a self-contained entity. It must relate to someone else to have any currency. To trust is to be conscious of someone else. It means to be vulnerable and to have someone else's vulnerability 'entrusted' to you. A quick glance at a dictionary will show that 'trust' is defined as 'faith' or in such qualities as 'reliability', 'honesty', 'integrity', 'truthfulness' or 'strength' of another person or thing.

So trust (or faith) will only be of any value to society and can only sustain a society if it is secure in a higher and more trust-worthy 'Other'. This is the reason why 70 per cent of people still believe in 'God' despite 200 years of a secular experiment. It is the driving force of all faiths. In the current cultural climate, trust is a timely focus, which should give Christians a great deal to talk about!

'Trust me, I'm a Christian'

As the people of a trusting and trustworthy God, you'd think 'trust' would be a value we had pinned down and an ideal foundation from which we appeal to the world. We might be able to trust others, and feel that we ourselves are trustworthy people, but the biggest hurdle to get over is the way others perceive us.

People are uncertain about the Church as an institution. The 1990 European Values Survey showed only 43 per cent of people trusting the Church, with just 30 per cent of eighteen to twenty-four year olds doing so. But there is clear evidence that church leaders still receive a level of trust from the people of Europe. So even though this trust fell from 85 per cent to 75 per cent between 1983 and 2004, the 2004 MORI poll showed that church leaders were still fourth in line after doctors, teachers and newsreaders. These are serious realities for Christian witness in the twenty-first century.

If it is to be taken seriously, the church has a major task on its hands. It has nothing to do with the nature of our message. In fact our highly spiritual culture, so fascinated by the paranormal could become increasingly open to our message. Any apparently ludicrous claim of Christian faith may now be put alongside the claims of all other faiths – as well as Satanists, spiritualists and atheists. The market-place is happy to listen to everyone and laugh at anyone.

The challenge of Christian witness has to do with authenticity: trustworthiness. People want to know if we are the real deal. This was true in the New Testament and it's true today. Many things stand between us and our trustworthiness. If we are to be heard and trusted we have some urgent items to attend to.

First, people must hear us expressing grace as much as truth. This is particularly true on issues such as human sexuality. Frankly, those who believe the historic view on human sexuality in general, and homosexuality in particular, are often among the most offensive people on the planet. Truth without grace is one way of keeping people away from grace. Those of us who hold to a conviction that practising homosexual acts are wrong are unlikely to win over the masses in the near future but we have an obligation to be a gracious and trustworthy minority.

Secondly, we will also have to own up to the atrocities that have taken place within the confines of the church. This applies particularly to the terrible examples of child abuse that have attracted so much attention in recent years. In this regard, the Christian church has been seriously indicted in the courts and in the press. When the current affairs flagship, the *Today* programme, conducted a debate on whether churches can be trusted to care for our children, we know we have a very real problem. Here we must measure the excellent work being done with young people alongside the clear recognition of where we have failed.

Third, churches have become synonymous with abuse of the vulnerable by the way in which we are perceived to exploit those in our care. In recent years we have become associated with high profile cases of financial mismanagement from established Anglican churches to independent charismatic churches. Churches with poor governance procedures or a strong message of 'prosperity' become particularly exposed in this regard.

When it comes down to it, our missionary task may not be that complicated. It begins, not with intellectual arguments about the nature or shape of church, a detailed awareness of cultural trends or bigger budgets, it begins with authentic communities whom people will listen to because we are trusted. And in our society, there has never been a more urgent need for trust as there is right now.

Of course, there is a host of other reasons for the general lack of trust in institutions that has come to typify our postmodern society. Infidelity, pathetic sermons detached from reality and poor public relations tend to distance us from our culture. And while these are genuine issues facing the church, they tell an unbalanced story, for the reality is that the majority of church professionals and attendees are trustworthy people. But even allowing for all this, these statistics are surely a wake-up call for an institution that should be seen above all others as trustworthy.

So, while we may ask ourselves whom we can trust, we should also ask from time to time, how trustworthy do others find us? And how can we become a more trusting society?

John Smith, UK director of the Evangelical Alliance offered some very helpful pointers in a Christian Resources Exhibition seminar in 2004:

> Safeguards may serve to protect us from the actions of others and may reduce our susceptibility to inappropriate behaviour which breaches trust. Yet alongside such safeguards that will inevitably and increasingly be imposed upon us, a look in the mirror may help us identify ways in which we may unwittingly and unintentionally abuse the trust that we hold.
>
> It's not hard to find examples. How many times have we readily offered to pray for someone, and failed to follow through? Better not to offer than to fail to deliver. Better still to deliver. In the area of guidance can we sometimes be over-confident and over-directive in declaring God's will for an individual?
>
> How many of us have allowed our bruised ego to suggest that their leaving our church fellowship may be accompanied by a reduction in God's personal blessing?

Am I always as objective as I might be in the tension between local church and kingdom or between my need to succeed and faithfulness to Christ's wider agenda? In my passion for Christ's cause do I sometimes make extreme claims in my advertising which actually are difficult to substantiate or justify? Do I find sometimes that even I am taken in by my own publicity? Self-delusion is the worst kind.

And what about the thorny issue of social action and proselytism? Do we care for people unconditionally out of a sense of compassion or have we always got an evangelistic purpose up our sleeve? How trustworthy are we when it comes to evangelism? Do we make the Christian life so easy to enter and paint it so rosy that we compromise the gospel of the one who spoke of a narrow way, of counting the cost, of self-denial? Do a person's troubles really come to an end when they trust Christ or would it be more honest to acknowledge that the struggle starts now?

Be real!

If you don't know, say so.

Don't hide your doubts and struggles.

Oh, and in the pastoral arena – never tell someone you know exactly how they feel – you can't possibly. You may share parallel experiences, but be aware of the limitation of comparison. Paul warned his assistant Timothy about some who would have the form of godliness but deny its power. We are often encouraged to practise what we preach, to walk the talk, but is there not a case for turning this around and saying if you want to preach with integrity only preach what you practise.

In recent years we have been encouraging Christians to take their place at the heart of a movement for change in contemporary Britain. Not only in terms of faith commitment and church attendance, but also in terms of crime, social exclusion, consumerism and sexual immorality. The UK is in desperate need of the gospel. Christian faith can draw on a rich legacy of transforming people's hearts, and transforming society in the name of Christ. But while commending such transformation to others, we won't get very far if we ourselves can't win their trust.

No doubt many of the spiritual and social problems which blight our nation today have their root in the breakdown of trust – between different classes and ethnic groups, parents and children, government and governed, bosses and workers, neighbours and colleagues. And there is no doubt that in Christ we have the greatest antidote to mistrust. Yet given the Church's own poor trust rating, it's more vital than ever that we return to the Scriptures and renew our understanding of what trust means from God's perspective. We have a responsibility to challenge ourselves but even more importantly, to point our world to a trustworthy Christ, because ultimately it is in him that people need to place their trust, not in God's erring children.

Trust in public and corporate life

Os Guinness' book *Doubt* begins with a helpful reminder that trust is indispensable to human relationships. Nothing works without it. From friendships between children to agreements among nations, life depends on trust. Counting on people is trust. Enjoying people is trust. Trust is the shared silence, the exchanged look, the expressive touch. Crying for help is trust, shaking hands is trust, a kiss is a sign of trust. The highest reaches of love and life depend on trust. All of these things are true.

But more than anything we need to understand, as individuals and as a nation, that trust is built. Writing in the *Sunday Times* in 2003 John Humphrys stated that, 'Trust is the cement in the democratic structure. Lose it and you lose power. Every politician knows that.' Once it is broken, trust is a slow if not impossible road to rebuild. And that's a frightening thought given the crises we are currently facing around the issue of trust in many of our most public institutions.

There is perhaps no more potent a story to demonstrate this than the death of Dr David Kelly and the subsequent inquiry by Lord Hutton. The Hutton Report and the Butler inquiry which investigated the Government's claims for going to war with Iraq are now synonymous with the issue of trust – the trust in our political leaders. At a personal level David Kelly trusted someone with information and that trust was apparently betrayed. But beneath the tragedy of human loss is a wider issue – the loss of trust at a national level.

Mistrust now runs deep in our society. Despite the assurances that Lord Hutton appeared to give us, it's inevitable that many will remain mistrustful of the government's reasons for taking us to war with Iraq. While Downing Street has been officially exonerated, even this may be insufficient to dispel the fundamental mistrust of a government which first swept to power on an anti-sleaze ticket and yet has become so tarred with a 'spin' brush that it overshadows any good that might be attempted.

Serious doubts too remain over the professionalism of the BBC – the broadcaster to which the nation has traditionally turned in times of crisis. Its reporting of this matter, and the unveiling of the insufficient editorial controls that allowed the *Today* programme report to be broadcast, may leave many with the question 'Can we still trust the BBC?'

Though less obvious to the general public, this culture of mistrust is also being mirrored in the corporate world. Trust in business is falling – across the EU 54 per cent of people say that they don't trust big companies. The financial institutions of the City of London formerly operated on the principle of 'my word is my bond' and a handshake was sufficient to seal a deal. As the level of trust that sustained that principle eroded, it has been replaced with a vast array of rules and supervisory bodies.

Again this is a serious issue. As Niall FitzGerald, chairman of Unilever, states, 'You can have all the facts and figures, all the supporting evidence, all the endorsements you want, but if – at the end of the day – you don't command trust, you won't get anywhere.' The business world is inconceivable without a trusting ethos. Indeed, studies have shown that the level of trust in a business affects its level of productivity. And when the corporate world throws up disasters such as Enron and Andersen, and figures show a significant growth in 'white collar' crime, this has far-reaching consequences for very ordinary people. In a consumerist society the erosion of trust in business is bad business for us all.

The Government's Corporate Social Responsibility programme launched on 5 July 2004 was an important innovation. It was effectively a recognition of the peculiar challenges facing the corporate world – a world in which the tension between corporate values and commercial interests meet. In this new initiative an alliance of major companies, including some of the big multinationals, will seek to encourage models of good practice that will strengthen trust in the corporate world.

Those of us who barely understand the entrepreneurial mind, there is a tendency to suspect anyone who handles or generates large sums of money and doesn't turn up regularly to mid-week services – unless, of course, they are contributing to the building fund! So the latent mistrust that many Christians have of people in business is fuelled by the high profile scandals that have become so commonplace in recent years.

In contrast, one of the positive signs of a renewed church today is the growth of Christian businessmen and women who are not only successful but clear that their business is their ministry. In the past two months I have met at least four such specimens of Christian disciples.

The business world has not suddenly become crooked. In fact good business people know that good values mean happy people and happy people mean productivity. It's far more complex. As a Christian businessman told me, in the fast-moving world where the interests of shareholders have to be measured against integrity, transparency and accountability, many companies simply lack the skills to keep up. Before they know it, they become a headline feature: failure to handle complex choices can lead to outcomes where trust is damaged.

When it comes down to it many of us face the same challenges. And it must have been the challenge Daniel faced in Babylon. But somehow he managed to keep his head – and his integrity. In fact, he was so reliable that even his accusers concluded that there was no fault or unfaithfulness in him (Dan. 6:4–5).

I hope Christian businesses will keep an eye on the Government's plans as they get off the runway. If the Corporate Social Responsibility programme goes some way to restoring that kind of trustworthiness in the world of business, it may be just another step or two towards more trusting relationships in the corporate world.

One answer to the lack of trust in society lies simply in allowing people to be more honest. Why is it so difficult for people in public life to say 'sorry' when they have so obviously made a mistake? Because they know the press and media will pillory them, because we have built a culture of blame instead of openness and forgiveness. And this has led to fear, which in turn stifles the possibility of building a culture of trust. We need to address the issue of the media and how it makes Pinocchios of our public servants. Our political leaders and public figures should be allowed legitimate margins of error. People should feel freer to admit mistakes without losing all credibility. Bad behaviour and bad decisions are not automatically exempted – we cannot stifle accountability in the public square. But we now need a political environment in which honesty, repentance and rehabilitation become possible. This is the only way to foster trust in the public square.

When Archbishop Rowan Williams decided it was necessary to add his voice to those concerned about this lack of trust in the public arena, he too found it hard not to be critical of our politicians. His speech implicated the Prime Minister with the erosion of public trust in Britain's political system. In his view, 'Government of whatever kind restores lost trust above all by its willingness to attend to what lies beyond the urgency of asserting control and retaining visible and simple initiative; by patient accountability and the freedom to think again, even to admit error or miscalculation.'

Archbishop Williams' controversial sermon, at St. Bebet's church in Cambridge in April 2004, posed a substantial challenge for political leaders. But unfortunately the deep cynicism in our culture means that admitting error or miscalculation alone is unlikely to bring the restoration of trust we all long to see. Mr Blair's U-turn on policy over a referendum on the European Constitution, which occurred at the same time as this sermon, made that quite clear. Furthermore the adversarial politics that led the Tory leader, Michael Howard, to mock Blair's change of heart, did little to restore public confidence in the business of politics. If Prime Ministers cannot reconsider, what hope is there for political transparency? Ironically, when Michael Howard taunted Blair, 'Who will ever trust you again?' it was not just an indictment on the Prime Minister, it was another nail in deflating our trust in politics.

Perhaps what we really need are the more measured thoughts of Clive Soley, MP and former chairman of the Parliamentary Labour Party, who in responding to Rowan Williams was recorded as saying that 'It is quite proper for anyone, including church leaders, to comment on the decline in trust in government . . . [But] we have to look deeper than single issues and we also have to look at the relationship between politicians and the media, where politicians are expected to never be wrong or to be very precise in their answers where the very nature of politics makes that difficult if not impossible.'

It is a fact hard to bear that more than ever our hope for our world has been sabotaged because trust in the trust-worthy has been so badly betrayed. But before we allow ourselves to raise our voices in criticism let's remind ourselves of *our* responsibilities in all this.

Restoring trust as a value in society

Restoring trust as a value respected throughout society will not be easy even though most people recognise how desperately we need it.

Christians who believe in a God who is trustworthy and trusts us have a distinct advantage. But it's an advantage we do not use well. If our appeal for a more trustworthy society is to be heard we must start with ourselves. And the first place to start is to follow Jesus' advice: 'Let your 'Yes' be 'Yes''. The most basic unit of trustworthiness is in the smallest expressions of human relationships. A trusted person in the home, workplace or on the sports field is an antidote to local cynicism. It is a powerful contribution to the restoration of our communities.

An old dictum says, we must 'dance at home before we dance abroad'. Marriage and family life is a key area and one in which the churches can help us, both emphasising the importance in marriage preparation of trust and in helping couples to maintain that trust through the ups and downs of married life.

Local churches are in an ideal place to be centres of trustworthiness. As part of the Evangelical Alliance's commitment to encourage churches to do this, our focus on trust has identified a number of key principles we ignore at the cost of the Gospel. But to restore trust we will need to review our values and draw from the virtues of the Spirit becoming 'salt and light' wherever we have an opportunity. We have not only to refrain from gazumping but also to challenge our friends and neighbours not to do it either. In conversation over a meal or a drink we can seek to persuade them that breaching trust is simply unacceptable. Similarly at work, we may achieve more by campaigning for a corporate ethos based on trust than, for example, by criticising a breach of trust after it has happened. While in large companies this may seem unrealistic if we are very junior, it may be possible to work through our trade union or staff association. We can point to the evidence that companies with a strong emphasis on trust tend to achieve better results.

We may think we are powerless to make any difference but it is worth noting the sort of people Jesus had in mind when he used the salt and light metaphors (Mt. 5:1–16). Paul van Buitnenen, the Christian who 'blew the whistle' on corruption in the European Commission, is a contemporary example for us of this.

Together we really can make a difference. We are powerless to influence the policies and practices of major companies if we try to act alone instead of drawing on the resources available to us in the Christian community. So for example, if we work in the business world we can link up with organisations like the Ridley Hall Foundation, the Jubilee Centre, the London Institute for Contemporary Christianity and the Business Group of the UCCF. Those working in one of the professions may find a specialist Christian group with which to campaign. The Lawyers' Christian Fellowship, the Christian Medical Fellowship and the Association of Christian Teachers are excellent examples. Teachers and School Governors can also make a common cause with CARE for Education and the Stapleford Centre.[6]

So far as politics is concerned, the challenge is to be prepared to review established voting loyalties in relation to the parties' trustworthiness record. CARE, Faithworks and the Evangelical Alliance are all committed to equipping churches to act prophetically in public policy and will give information and advice. Each of the major political parties has a Christian Group: the Christian Socialist Movement, the Conservative Christian Fellowship and the Liberal Democrat Christian Forum. They should all be open to dialogue about restoring and maintaining trust in British politics and society.

In the present scenario politicians seem helpless to tell the truth and need the help of the public. So trust demands a new approach to corporate responsibility in which the public takes responsibility to create the public servants we need. In a liberal democracy we don't just get the politicians we *deserve*, we get the public figures we create. We have 650 MPs and 40 million voters. We are the empowered majority. All of us have a responsibility to encourage circumstances that promote dependability in public servants. If we simply believed that all politicians are the same and gave up on them then our democracy would collapse. Politicians need to be trusted, and we need to take the opportunities to let them know that they are, not just for their own good, but also for the good of us all.

Trusting is about putting people at the centre. Politicians are people too! Write to them in support when they are seen to be honest and trustworthy. Thank them for doing their job well. Rather than believing that they are always bad people, why not challenge the press and opinion-formers about the stories they write up as facts? Press media has huge responsibility, power and influence. More than ever in a liberal democracy it reflects and shapes public opinion. When opinion-formers act without integrity they dislodge delicate particles that hold society together and can start landslides in our culture.

But if you are unable to exercise trust in your political figures, the Christian option is not to resort to apathy. Instead, see your purpose as fighting for change and the creation of a new era of good and trustworthy politicians. Pray for politicians and the political system. If you believe yourself to be a trustworthy person, and that others will see that value in you, then why not participate in the political process? Even protest is healthier than cynicism.

The media also has a part to play. The letters columns and the feedback programmes on radio and television are there for Christians to use just like anyone else. To be effective it helps if we write courteously, concisely and in a language and style intelligible to those we seek to influence. In this and any other form of campaigning it is essential for Christians to remain close to Christ through prayer, Bible study and fellowship with other believers. This is not a pietistic cliché; it is to ensure that we do God's will, in God's way, and for his glory.

If life without trust is unbearable, nobody wants it. That means that if trust is being eroded it is hurting people. If we can persuade them that it does not have to be like this then they are likely to be on our side even if they do not share the Christian faith. This is a door worth opening to restore trust, and it could also lead some to faith.

APPLICATION

1. Have you succumbed to cynicism and apathy?
2. What can you do to reverse the trend?

Two

Hope – the Answer to Cynicism

Hope is . . . the inescapable companion of faith.
(Jürgen Moltmann, *Theology of Hope*)

Always be prepared to give an answer to everyone who
asks you to give the reason for the hope that you have.
(1 Pet. 3:15)

Working into the night

There is a tendency in Christian ministry to appeal to
disaster as a prelude to salvation. In other words, we
need to make people feel bad before we make them feel
good. We are always in danger, therefore, of sounding
like undertakers at a birthday party! So even if we
struggle with it, we have to admit that a part of our
prophetic role is to leave room to celebrate the good in
our world. The earth is still the Lord's and everything in
it (Ps. 24:1). And in spite of our spiritual, political and
cultural chaos, his glory still fills the whole earth (Is. 6:3).

On the whole, we enjoy the merits and the challenges
of a more tolerant society. People still respond to

charitable causes. We still resent injustice and unveiled aggression. We still see the vestiges of the image of God struggling for recognition in our behaviour.

There is still a reservoir of kindness in our culture. A golden thread of goodwill runs through the fabric of our society. We are privileged to stand on the highest point of technological and scientific achievement. There is poverty in Britain, but generally we have 40 per cent more disposable income than we did 10 years ago. Fifteen years ago, Britain had 6600 millionaires; today we have well over 47,000.

Christians are not bad-news merchants, but as the reformer Martin Luther once said, we may have to know God as an enemy before we know him as a friend. So inevitably Christians have a responsibility to flag up ways in which our fallen nature damages human relationships. And the fact is that we are called to point out signs of decay in our society.

For example, in one month – September 2003 – there were 66,000 recorded acts of anti-social behaviour committed. Overall crime figures had fallen but violent crimes were up and gun crime had risen by three per cent. In spite of our relative wealth and affluence, the second highest cause of death for young men under twenty-five is suicide. Teenage pregnancy and sexually transmitted diseases are reaching serious proportions in Britain today.

And when we set that alongside the growing anxieties of our farming community or pensioners whose world is collapsing with the financial markets, it's little wonder that there is so much dismay around. World affairs have only served to compound our growing sense of vulnerability in the world. Iraq, the Middle East and Northern Ireland. Terrorism and terror, Saddam Hussein and Osama bin Laden have become labels we use to summarise our restlessness in the twenty-first century.

Calling its name

In January 2003 I attended a gun summit convened by the Home Secretary after the brutal murder of two young women in Aston, Birmingham. During the meeting a senior police officer made a memorable statement. 'What we need,' he said, 'are exit routes from the hopelessness facing our young people.' Not long after, I met with the chief of police in the West Midlands. When I asked for an explanation on why young people shot each other in order to gain respect, his answer was quite simple: 'A lack of hope.'

When a small group of scholars met with Walter Brueggemann to discuss global missions, their consensus paper which serves as a prelude in *Hope for the World* made it very clear that, 'the prevailing mood of humankind, globally considered, must be named "despair".'[7]

Christian witness does not consist of telling people they are unhappy when they are not. But we do need to point out that you can still be happy and hopeless. It is perfectly possible to be hopelessly happy.

Here is a good example in our own lifetime. 'I sit in my house in Buffalo and sometimes I get so lonely it's unbelievable. Life has been so good to me. I've got a great wife, good kids, money, my own health – and I'm lonely and bored.' That was O. J. Simpson in June 1988.

The road to reality is paved with true reminders. And as Pete Lowman put it, 'The Titanic's cooking was superb, but it didn't make up for their failure to notice the icebergs.'[8]

Wells of despair

But even though it may be hard to see it in our present situation, our highpoint of hopelessness was not on

11 September 2001. It was not on 1 January 2003. The highpoint of our hopelessness was at the point, many years ago, when we told ourselves that humankind had come of age and that God was dead. When our philosophers killed God six generations ago we began a new descent into death. When we 'killed God' we set sail on a journey about which the only thing we were certain was that we didn't know where we were going. Six generations later, the catchphrase of the twenty-first century has become 'I don't know!'

Neitzche, a great grandfather of our present despair put it like this: 'Where are we moving to? Away from all suns? Are we not running incessantly? Backwards, sideways and forwards, in all directions? Is there still an above and a below? Are we not wandering through an infinite nothingness? Has it not become colder?'[9]

You don't have to be a philosopher and you don't have to be good at maths to work out this equation: nothingness leads to no-oneness. And, more than ever before, our sense of hopeless and no-oneness has led to another problem. It's not only multiple personality disorders we fear, it's a kind of neutral personality disorder. A sense of nobodiness. A spiritual vacuum in which people have a lot to live with, but little to live for.

The horrors of two world wars left us vulnerable and shaken. The revolution of the 1960s was the backlash of our fears. We feared 'the bomb'. We learned new words like 'Polaris missiles' and 'Trident submarines' and feared things only politicians and dictators controlled.

We were still afraid in the 1990s. *Panorama* called it the 'decade of despair'. People under forty feared HIV and Aids. People over forty feared the insecurity of unemployment. Everybody began to fear for our environment. And in hopelessness we queued up to watch *Deep Impact* and *Independence Day*.

When we celebrated our new millennium no one saw what was coming. Bin Laden is now a household name. Today, any film with the Twin Towers of the World Trade Center is seriously dated. We have discovered that terror and terrorism don't need passports. New York or North London. Afghanistan or Aston. It really doesn't matter.

Looking for hope

There is a question that underlies our cultural mood: Where do we look for hope and a sense of identity? The search for meaning is an urgent quest in our culture. And it has been made much harder by a society that has moved away from its Judaeo-Christian values and its deep distrust of historic institutions. Our alternatives include sexual licence, materialism, leisure or work. But all the evidence suggests that these are turning out to be poor substitutes for souls restless without God.

You don't have to be a naïve idealist in order to be a Christian! We know that we are in a fallen world that will never know perfection until all things are finally made new. But neither are Christians pessimists. We are called to be people of hope in a world of hopelessness. Indeed, our primary calling to be salt and light is essentially a calling to be the people of hope.

So we need something different. We need another message. And it has to be a message of hope. As Alister McGrath put it, 'Only by rediscovering its theology of hope can the church hope to gain a hearing in a secular culture.'[10]

We need a message that takes seriously the resurrection of God in the common consciousness and a new understanding of who we were meant to be. God by his own description is 'the God of hope' (Rom. 15:13, Acts 24:15). Everything about God speaks of irrepressible hope. So even when we 'killed him', he refused to die. Hope really does spring eternal! You cannot keep a good God down! The God of the Bible is alive and hopeful in our pain. He's listening to the conversations about the future. The God of hope doesn't wait for the skies to clear in order to show up. He doesn't wait for the grand finale. He is there in the rehearsals when we're trying to get it right. He is there in the arguments and shared perspectives.

As Botman states, 'Real faithful embrace of hope does not arise from the ashes of a natural theology or from divine historical precedence but from the awakening to a hope for a future that is manifested in the very idea that God has a future.'[11]

A message about people

The message we have to offer is this: there is hope. And it begins with a recognition of who we are. There is an underlying culture of passive death that erodes hope in our world. It begins with our freedom to quietly destroy 600 babies every day in England and Wales and ends up with high profile shootings on our streets. But God has a high view of us. When God looks at us he sees people fallen but made in his own image. When God thinks about you he doesn't start with an amoeba or monkey and work upwards. He begins with himself and works outwards.

During my work as a North London probation officer in the 1980s, I had a nineteen-year-old client called Eddie. Eddie was an extravagant dresser who would usually visit me draped in gold and silk. At any one time Eddie could be valued in excess of £4000–£5000! One day I asked him why he was dressed so extravagantly. His answer was memorable. 'If I don't wear my stuff,' he said, 'I'm nothing.' There are thousands of people who believe that about themselves today.

But people who believe that they are made in the image of God are likely to place a very different value on themselves. They become more than they own or wear. They become more than the car they drive. And they become more than we can snatch from someone else on a street corner.

Hope in the public square

We need to convey an urgent message for opinion formers. And it is this: people can become what they watch. We must refuse to accept the notion that watching hours of violence and obscenity makes no difference. If our television and media has no measurable impact on our children's minds, then someone needs to tell that to the advertising and marketing industries.

There is a massive challenge facing all of us as we observe the huge influence of the MTV culture which is designed to tell young people that their value as people is defined entirely in materialistic, short-term bursts of high-flying lifestyles and disposable relationships.

And we need a message of hope to pass on to Government. Good government will resist the seduction of sensational journalists who think hope means more overcrowded prisons. If being tough on the causes of crime includes a National Policing Policy that makes the community critical partners with the police, than that is what we must do. If being tough on the causes of crime means more schemes like Splash Extra and Community Award Schemes which help young people experience that there is a world beyond their neighbourhood, then this is what we must do.

The get-tough policies of the past 20 years have done nothing to give us hope. The Margaret Thatcher era of 'short, sharp shock' did nothing to stem the tide of criminality, and today, the jury is still out on 'tough on crime and tough on the causes of crime'. Hope doesn't tiptoe around injustice. Hope which works may not immediately win votes but it is the better option. It doesn't matter if it seems soft as long as it works and brings hope.

Hope and the message of the Church

We need a new message to the Church. The Christian message of hope works from a particular script. It's the promise of hope that begins with the forgiveness of our sin and sinfulness through faith in Jesus Christ. It ends with the promise of eternal life in the presence of God who will renew all things bringing them under the control of his Son. It's a point of view that sometimes attracts ridicule, but one to which orthodox Christian faith remains committed. For between the promise of personal forgiveness and the renewal of all things, hope is still at work. Christians work because we care and because we also hope.

In fact, the hope of the Church is its most prophetic impulse for action. In the apostle Paul's contention, hope fuels our resolve in tough situations (Rom. 5:3–5). As Moltmann insists, 'Those who hope in Christ can no longer put up with reality as it is, but begin to suffer under it, to contradict it. Peace with God means conflict with the world for the goad of the promised future stabs inexorably into the flesh of every unfaithful present . . . This hope makes the Christian Church a constant disturbance in human society, seeking as the latter does to stabilize itself into a continuing city.'[12]

Sadly, we have not been heard to be a people of hope. People think of Christians for other reasons. But hope is central to our calling. We must talk about sin and forgiveness because no one else will. But we must also talk about redemption, love and hope. We must not suffocate hope by our traditions and our important in-house debates.

We have a lot more to do but we also have a story to tell about what we are doing to bring hope. Churches employ twice the amount of youth workers as local governments do. And we do it because we have hope. We do have a quiet and growing campaign of hope being carried out in numerous church groups and organisations. Today, 29 per cent of Christians are involved in voluntary work compared with nine per cent in society.

Human life and the concept of community are utterly impossible without hope. This is true because hope always reaches beyond ourselves to 'the other'. Hope creates interdependence. This is why people without hope seldom ask for other people's help.

So hope is not afraid of awkward situations. Hope does not pretend. Real hope weeps with those who weep. It fears neither death nor despair. Hope allows us to be angry without becoming bitter. And as Bauckham and Hart suggest, 'Even in the most difficult and threatening of situations hope "is always slow to admit that all the facts are in, that all the doors have been tried and that it is defeated".'[13]

Hope never gives up; it has a tendency to ignore the final whistle and plays into extra time. Hope is not an option for society; it is a necessity. Without hope we die a thousand deaths. Without it, we cannot legislate or police our streets. Without hope our communities stumble from one shooting to another and from one public inquiry to the next. Without hope a nation has no common language with which to discuss its future existence. As Martin Luther King Jnr put it, 'even in the inevitable moments when all seems hopeless, men know that without hope they cannot really live.'[14]

Hope is greater than the human spirit because it belongs to God. It propels us up beyond ourselves and our circumstances into God's eye-view of the world. And that is the best place from which to see the world and become involved in it.

Practising hope

When we first raised Hope as a value worth restoring to society, a number of things became clearer to me. First, there are already a great number of hope-filled activities happening in many Christian communities. In 2000 the Report from the Christian Research Association showed that even in the face of declining attendance, 42 per cent of Christian churches carry out non-proselytising acts of kindness as an integral part of their Christian witness.

But I am also becoming increasingly aware that hope is being carried beyond the walls of our churches through powerful evangelistic tools such as *Alpha* and *Christianity Explored*. It is reflected in the imaginative way J. John has brought the relevance of the Ten Commandments to our culture in powerful evangelistic campaigns. I see this hope rekindled in Christian witness and action in youth organisations such as Crusaders and Youth for Christ or the work of The Message and Soul Survivor. In all these examples clear messages about hope in Christ are being accompanied by lives that have been changed through encounters with Jesus Christ and the God of hope.

Far more importantly, it is happening through acts of hope in countless local churches. Sir Fred Catherwood's *It Can Be Done* and the *Faithworks* series give brief catalogues of such encouraging stories available to us across the landscape of Christian witness. That hope is also communicated at ground level through other established ministries such as Christian Aid, Shaftesbury, the Church Urban Fund and the YMCA.

While we become increasingly anxious about headlines detailing the decline of the Christian church, governments and decision-makers are increasingly aware of the role of faith and the Christian church in social care. Most of our historic churches, such as Catholic, Anglican, and Methodist have a long history of social responsibility. Denominational and independent Christian relief and development agencies have also caught the attention of policy makers and governments as being serious partners in the fight against injustice and poverty. The Christian Church was, for example, at the heart of the debt campaign, Jubilee 2000, and won the clear recognition of the Chancellor and Minister for International Development. As I write, I am also aware of the global movement against poverty that is being developed by Christian organisations involved in the Micah Challenge.[15]

In July and August 2004 some 15,000 young people worked with over 750 churches for one of the most ambitious and challenging missions which combined evangelism with multiple acts of kindness across the capital called Soul in the City. The mission was an outstanding example of hope in action. But the mission also aimed to bring 'lasting change by giving people involved such a positive model of mission that they would be inspired to make evangelism a way of life for life'.

Through youth agencies, disability schemes, policing safer communities and local and mayoral elections, the Christian church is raising its act to become not just messenger of hope, but a hope-bringer.

The Church has a lot to live up to. But in its own quiet way it is seeking to live up to a lot. Our message of hope will only really be carried out if we are first confident of the urgency of this mission and aware of the extent to which we are already involved. But we must also realise just how much more there is to be done in a world hunting for hope.

As we approached Christmas 2003 a rather attractive leaflet from a local church came through my door. I recognised the artwork on the front from our publications on hope. On the back of the leaflet I was being invited to a special Christmas service. I received two subsequent invitations, one inviting me to come and hear a professional psychiatrist addressing the needs in my local area and a second asking me to join them in doing something about rising gun crimes. Here was faith and hope in action.

APPLICATION

1. Consider your fellowship/church. Is it 'in its own quiet way seeking to live up to a lot'? Or is the focus primarily on meeting the needs of its members?
2. How involved *are* we?

Three

Love Me – Respect Me

> Love is patient, love is kind. It does not envy, it does not boast, it is not proud. It is not rude, it is not self-seeking, it is not easily angered, it keeps no record of wrongs. Love does not delight in evil, but rejoices with the truth. It always protects, always trusts, always hopes, always perseveres. (1 Cor. 13:4–7)

As I wrote this chapter, the treatment of Iraqi prisoners by coalition troops was the constant headline of the printed and broadcast news. Images of degrading humiliation and psychological torture filled our waking hours. Debates raged as to whether these prisoners deserved any respect, given their part in upholding one of the most brutal regimes of all times. But, equally, President Bush's campaigning rhetoric that the war in Iraq was 'a fight between the civilised nations of the developed world and an axis of evil based around the Middle East' seemed to lose all its currency overnight. What little respect that may have been gained in ousting a brutal dictator was irretrievably lost. The traumatic and shocking images of the last moments and beheading of Nick Berg, an American civilian taken captive while on business in Iraq, provided a graphic illustration of a lack of mutual respect.

Thankfully this is an extreme event in our world. But these images are also the wake-up call signalling that respect is a value that, when lost, can lead us to extremes of inhumanity and utter depravity. Loss of respect may find its pinnacle in such actions but spreading out below them is inter-gang violence on the streets of Britain's cities. Religious intolerance. Anti-social behaviour. Social exclusion. Street robbery. Sexual abuse. Sexual harassment. Discrimination. Bullying. In short, respect is a foundational value on which to build safe, supportive and flourishing communities. A point not lost on Tony Blair when he spelt out his vision for Britain back in 2002:

> Respect is a simple notion. We know instinctively what it means. Respect for others – their opinions, values and way of life. Respect for neighbours; respect for the community that means caring about others. Respect for property, which means not tolerating mindless vandalism, theft and graffiti. And self-respect, which means giving as well as taking. Respect is at the heart of a belief in society. It is what makes us a community, not merely a group of isolated individuals.

Respect your neighbour – as yourself

Respect was a biblical idea long before it became a street word. The biblical idea of respect underpins our relationship not only with God but also with other people. In fact the absence of respect for God is an indicator that we are heading in the wrong direction (Is. 5:12; Mal. 1:6). But the Bible is equally concerned about the lack of

mutual respect between people. Leadership is particularly singled out as deserving of respect (Deut. 1:13). In
fact, our liberal democracy should take particular note
of the biblical model in this text, for in this passage, the
people first chose leaders from their tribes who they
respected and who God then appointed over them.
Special emissaries are identified with the mark of
respect – as in the story of the vineyard owner recorded
in the Synoptic Gospels (Mt. 21:37; Mk. 12:6 and
Lk. 20:13). Similarly, key characters who acted as hinges
in God's plans for the early church were marked by
respect (Acts 10:22; 22:12).

Biblical respect is also attached to marital and
parental relationships (Lev. 19:3; Eph. 5:33; 1 Pet. 3:7; 1
Tim. 3:4), the elderly and young, (Deut. 28:50; Prov. 5:12)
and slaves and regulated attitudes between servants and
masters (Eph. 6:5; 1 Tim. 6:1; 1 Pet. 2:8). And beyond
these in-house relationships, God expects respect to be
extended to our wider relationships as part of Christian
witness to a watching world (1 Thes. 4:12). This is particularly true for Peter who challenged a persecuted
church to have an 'apology' for the hope of their faith
offered with 'gentleness and respect.' (1 Pet. 3:15–16).

Biblical respect, however, should never be confused
with the idea of benign accommodation or the passive
tolerance of another human being. Biblical respect is
tough. It is invariably linked with the idea of fear or
trepidation. Respect for God is therefore dependent on
an element of fear. The fear of God is the gateway to wisdom. Similarly, the vineyard owner who sent his son to
deal with the workers was expected to command
'respect' (*entrepo*). The Greek word actually means to
engender shame or regard. This was precisely why the
owner would have been shocked and angry about the
murder of his son at the hands of the workers. So when

Peter encouraged his readers to talk about hope with 'gentleness and respect', the word (*phobia*) translates as 'fear' (1 Pet. 3:15,16).

So does this mean that the Bible expects human relationships to be driven by fear? Not for a moment. As W. Mundle points out, 'The New Testament presents a tension between fear and love. In a paradoxical way, they go together.'[16]

Biblical fear is divine respect. True love expels terrified fear and opens up the door to a reverential respect for God. But it also inspires a sacred respect for others made in God's image. Love, which never fails, desires the very best for the other and usually begins with respect. This is why people who love each other are actually *afraid* to hurt each other.

Respect yourself!

As we raise the profile of 'respect' as an integral part of our Values campaign, we see it as a critical point of contact with our culture in the twenty-first century. The rest of this chapter will raise thoughts and questions, stimulate dialogue and encourage the Christian community and society to enforce the importance and relevance of 'respect' as we journey deeper into the new millennium.

'You cannot hope to be respected by others unless you respect yourself' is now a bench-mark quote. But more than that, if you lack self-respect then the chances are you won't properly respect others either. Indeed, the Belgian-born writer, Maurice Maeterlinck once noted, 'If you love yourself meanly, childishly, timidly, even so shall you love your neighbour.' That we love and respect ourselves is the prelude to the kind of love that transforms society by reaching out to the 'other' from the security of our own self-respect. Self-love rather than selfish love is a prerequisite for a healthy society. And in a culture where self-harm has become endemic for young people, self-respect is an urgent notion which needs to be heard.

But aside from such philosophical ideas and social advancements, self-respect has been turned from a value at the heart of strong, vital communities into a 'be-good-to-yourself' culture – the one single idea that drives our advertising industry more than any other. The primacy of the self and its satisfactions is everything in our world. That we love ourselves and respect ourselves should be self-evident (so the advertisers tell us) from the food we eat, the clothes we wear, the places we live, where we go on holiday, the car we drive and the people we mix with – after all, 'You're worth it'.

Go into any high street newsagent and scan the content of the popular magazines or turn on the TV most mornings of the week and you can see this popular philosophy at work in an infinite array of adverts, articles, self-help editorials and day-time shows. And yet the irony is that they show less and less respect for the kind of mundane lives most of us live. What's really respected is wealth, beauty, celebrity, notoriety and youth. In such an environment, how are we really supposed to feel confident about our worth and about the regard in which we are held? How is the ordinary person really supposed to find the self-respect needed to give and receive the respect of others? Is there any wonder our therapy has to be person-centred?

The absence of self-respect can bring pain and sorrow to our lives. We are at our most vulnerable when our self-respect is gone. But we can also be at our most aggressive. So, for example, in the corporate setting, any 'self-respecting' management guru will tell you that, 'respect is commanded not demanded'. But if our self-respect breaks down or is taken from us, then our instinct seems to be to rob others of their self-respect also. Power and hierarchy are then used as weapons rather than tools of productivity and mutual benefit. Those in power who crave the respect of their staff but fear they don't have it, mimic it by bullying those underneath them. The need to regain self-respect blinds us from the damage we do to others and we end up with a total collapse in respect.

The human, social and economic cost of our lack of mutual and self-respect is enormous. If our industries and work places were truly concerned with productivity and staff welfare then they would be trying hard to maintain the self-respect of every individual they employ. Without it, all they produce is wasted emotional energy, the destruction of confidence and creativity, and alienation.

We need to reclaim the value of self-respect from the advertisers and we need to be pro-active in generating mutual self-respect in our daily relationships. We cannot allow the media and institutions to determine the social fabric of our nation. We need to find ways to re-establish self-respect and consideration towards the people around us based on more than a 'be-good-to-yourself' mantra. The value of self-respect helps us to feel less threatened by the world around us and more able to take an active part in shaping it.

Respect your neighbours

'R.E.S.P.E.C.T.' sang the soul legend Aretha Franklin, challenging her listeners to find out what it means. In a multi-ethnic, culturally diverse Britain there may be no more pertinent a challenge. What does it mean to 'respect' someone of African-Caribbean descent? How is respect shown in an Islamic culture? For the Buddhist or the Hindu, how is respect articulated? What does it mean to have respect as a white Anglo-Saxon male?

Certainly in recent years there have been many laudable attempts to meet with our neighbour, to respect them and their culture. One such annual event is the Respect Festival, which has been running now for a number of years in London (though there are similar events in most major cities in the UK). What this has shown us is that to truly respect our neighbour we have to understand their culture – and that means gaining an understanding by engaging with their art, literature, music, religion, politics and values.

But in reality, these events are becoming less and less about understanding a diverse culture and reducing racism through bringing disparate races together – learning to love my 'strange' neighbour – and more about the expression of who we believe we are – people comfortable with our own mixed identity.

In the last census (the first to allow people to select a clear ethnic identity) one million people in Britain declared themselves to be of more than one race or of no particular race. It's now thought that by the next census, those covered by the term 'mixed race', currently the third largest minority group in Britain, will be the largest. Black British, Asian British, British Asian, White European – we have diversity to the 'nth degree'. But such diversity isn't clarifying boundaries but blurring them. We live, not so much in a multicultural society but as multicultural individuals. And this is equally true whether we are born to ethnically diverse parents or, as is increasingly the case, we simply choose to take on diversity in our lifestyles.

'Forget Black. Forget White. EA is What's Hot!' Imagine my surprise on reading this headline one Sunday morning in *The Observer*. Finally the press had come to their senses and seen the reality that had been staring them in the face all along – being part of the EA is where it's at. But like the biggest present under the tree at Christmas, surprise often turns to disappointment when you unwrap it and discover the reality.

The point of the article written by John Arlidge, wasn't to sing the praises of the Evangelical Alliance, but to flag up a phenomenon: Generation EA – Ethnically Ambiguous. You see it in music and fashion, and you experience it on the streets. For many young people, black urban culture has become the mainstream culture. White youngsters are deliberately adopting the fashion, lifestyle, music and language of the black community. But it's more nuanced than that. Popular music artists such as the rapper Eminem, Justin Timberlake, Beyoncé and Christine Aquilera all merge cultural and ethnic identities through visual image, music sampling and lifestyle. With Beckham, famously voted the most famous Black Man in Britain, they are the role models that reflect and project image and cultural identity for millions of young people on both sides of the Atlantic.

Multi-cultural Britain is a reality. According to the Office of National Statistics, seven per cent of people in Britain are 'non-white'. Between 1992–1994 the 'ethnic' population grew from 3.2 to 3.7 million. And from 1997–1999 it grew by 15.6 per cent compared with a 'white' population growth of one per cent. Today's London is 34 per cent black. Given the present rate of growth there has been a prediction that Britain will have a majority 'ethnic' population by 2100.

Understandably, trend analysts are fascinated by the rise of these racial hybrids. Peter Howatt, former editor of *Esquire* magazine, has observed that 'the racially-indeterminate melting pot aesthetic is very "now".' But this goes deeper than mere music and fashion – it goes to the heart and soul of what it means to live in the UK in the early twenty-first century.

But that doesn't mean we have entered into a utopian society of mutual respect, where to look at my neighbour means to gaze into a mirror. Issues and questions surrounding respect are still being fought on a daily basis. While the majority find it harder than ever to hold a 'them and us' attitude within our communities in terms of race and ethnic boundaries, there has been a steady rise of hardliners joining extremist groups and right-wing political parties such as the BNP. In our schools dozens of teachers are leaving every year because of the lack of respect they receive. Anti-social orders are on the increase. And we all have to face the question: what does it means to respect elders and the elderly in a youth-driven culture?

The old adage 'people don't care how much you know until they know how much you care' is certainly very true of the younger generation. This might be the reason why traditional authority figures are generally less respected by this generation. 'Why should I respect the police, the government, my teachers? What have they ever done for me?' This is also probably why friendships are valued so heavily – often more so than family relationships. Friendships, though sometimes rocky, cultivate loyalty, commitment, understanding and belonging. These things contribute to a mutual respect and appreciation.

Respecting outsiders

As the last section suggests, 'outsiders' is a shifting category. If I were writing this 50 years ago, even 15 years ago, I may well be thinking of myself as an 'outsider'. As a black person in Britain I am aware that Black and ethnic groups are significantly disadvantaged in multi-cultural Britain. Even so, our response to the inequalities we experience is from the perspective from those who belong: as 'insiders'. But in Britain there are still many outsiders. Outsiders are often refugees, asylum seekers or travellers. In a recent Channel Four programme *Who you callin AN?*, Black African-Caribbeans clearly regarded Somali youth as the outsiders. In our society, outsiders can be disabled people or the mentally ill.

Respect is a 'chicken-egg' question. Do we earn respect, or is it something given to us that we either keep or lose? And in giving respect do we then earn it? The truth is, we should give respect to another human being freely, without judgement. We should presume the goodness of the 'outsider' rather than their depravity. Judgement should be withheld until we truly know an individual. Respect and hope are values that go hand in hand – we respect our fellow human beings in the hope that they prove to be worthy of that respect.

If we are truly to call ourselves a tolerant society, then we cannot judge ourselves by the respect given to those among us who are familiar, but to those who are strangers and 'outsiders'. We must learn to look with hope when we look at those on the margins, those excluded from our 'tolerant' and 'respecting' communities, because today's stranger is tomorrow's friend.

A Christian response

Setting our house in order

No Christian response to respect can begin unless we are prepared to model what it means among us. Christians are people with deep-seated convictions and strong passions. Truth and traditions matter a great deal to us. Sometimes, it appears, more than grace, courtesy and respect. A watching world is unlikely to believe that we have much respect for each other if they are besieged by complicated theological debate about our important in-house issues.

The time has come to vet our public debates on matters such as human sexuality rather more carefully – without compromising our convictions. At the height of this debate, I was invited to appear on a well-known TV programme. Having agreed to participate I then discovered that the subject was homosexuality. I agreed, feeling that I had little to add to our well-publicised, historic views on the subject. I was then told I would be in debate with another Christian leader on the subject. I declined. It wasn't a nervousness to debate the issue with a differing Christian viewpoint. It was simply that I had no appetite to feed the media frenzy that has little interest in clarifying theological positions but much to gain from public controversy.

Christians need to give an answer for their hope with 'gentleness and respect' (1 Pet. 3:15,16). This applies as much to the heated debates across the Protestant/Catholic divides in Northern Ireland as it does between the charismatic/non-charismatic debates in the Christian press. I am still alarmed at the Christian propensity to be rude in the name of God. To parade truth in the absence of grace. This applies particularly to parts of the Christian press that belittle others without personal contact. The Christian press must live up to its responsibilities in this regard and Christian preachers must present Christ confidently, without disrespect to other Christian groups or by vilifying other faiths.

Seeing people differently

When Jesus was asked the question, 'Who is my neigh-bour?' (Lk. 10:29) his answer was more than a surprise to the religious leaders of his day; it was a complete shock. And we need to understand why, if we are to grasp and mirror the way Jesus approached respect.

We love to tell this story as a parable of surprise – sur-prise that it was the hated person who helped out. Perhaps we would replace the Samaritan with an asylum seeker, for instance, if we were to retell it for our age. But to understand what Jesus was really saying, we need to go back to the conversation that occurs prior to the parable.

The real agenda wasn't about social action but about eternal life – the inheritance of the Kingdom of God and how that can be achieved – by loving God and loving my neighbour (Lk. 10:25–27). But then who is my neighbour? Where do the boundaries lie? After all, some people – sinners and the like – are surely beyond the expectations of such a command?

What Jesus does in telling this parable the way he does is to explode all possible boundaries for the extent of God's love and, therefore, ours. What the Pharisee asking the question was looking for was boundary setting – preferably comfortable ones. What he got was a neighbour for whom he held no love and no respect. The person who fulfilled the requirements for entry into the Kingdom of God represented the most despised and disrespected person Jesus could think of.

This parable fits well our need for respect. It demon-strates to us the need to respect ourselves, to respect the neighbour we know and with whom we share our lives, but also to respect the outsider. For God has placed no limits on his love for us, so we must place no limits on our love for others, whoever they may be.

We also need to learn that to respect someone isn't just to acknowledge from afar some virtue they might have. Respect is more than words; it is a pro-active decision to love others as I am first loved. As we saw earlier, to respect is to love. To truly grasp this, it might help to hear Jesus speak to us all in a familiar way, but in the light of the story of the Good Samaritan, with a justifiable twist:

> A new command I give you: Respect one another. As I have respected you, so you must respect one another. By this all men will know you are my disciples, if you respect one another.   (Jn. 13:34–35, paraphrase)

The Christian faith has an acute challenge at its doorstep. Not only are we called to evaluate our response to our emerging neighbours, but we are also faced with the new challenge of other faiths in a country that has been historically regarded as a 'Christian country'. A Christian response to the particular challenges of Islam or other faiths cannot and should not be combative. It must first be characterised by love and respect. Christian witness in the twenty-first century will be tested by its respect for others even more than its orthodoxy.

Respect is not another word for compromise. Respect involves a Christian responsibility to ensure that all legitimate faiths have a right to be heard in Britain, but it does not mean throwing Christian distinctives overboard. The basis of our claims about the uniqueness of Christ will depend on our right to be heard and not on our claims to history.

Respect and youth culture

A recent discussion with the Chief Constable of the West Midlands made it clear that respect is high on the agenda for many young people today. And this goes beyond a simple pat of two fists to the shout of 'Rrrrespect!' For young black people particularly, disrespect ('dissing'), even among themselves, is a serious step over the mark when it comes to social interaction. Such anti-values can even lead to killing. In the Metropolitan Police's Trident programme, six per cent of murders (primarily within the black community) are generated by a 'lack of respect'.

Given the chronic levels of anti-social behaviour (over 6000 incidents were recorded in one day in September 2003) it is not surprising that 'respect' along with themes of hope, trust and responsibility have been included in our School curriculum. It is an open invitation for churches, youth groups and school workers to respond with relevance and effectiveness to the values vacuum in our youth culture.

It is clear that giving respect results in receiving respect in due course. Over breakfast with a Christian policeman I heard a very powerful example of this. As an inspector, my police friend took the trouble to build one-to-one relationships with young men on his patch. Then one evening he drove up to the area where they met. As the car approached the group dispersed. But as he got out of the vehicle and they recognised him, they all came back to talk with him. It was clear that firstly they weren't doing anything wrong. But secondly, his respect for them meant that they were able to review their views of and relationship to the police service.

In May 2004 a secondary school arranged an abortion for a fifteen-year-old student without her parents' awareness. Whatever the legality of the school's position, this is simply a disastrous contribution to a culture already struggling to make sense of parent-children relationships – particularly cases where relationships were otherwise harmonious.

When respect goes missing in our homes, parental orders for truanting children become the inevitable choice. In such instances the law becomes no more than a poor restraint in the absence of self-regulating values.

Christian witness has an urgent contribution to make to parent-children relationships. And there is much more we can do. Think of the time, expertise and good models we have at our disposal. What could we accomplish if our Sunday schools and youth groups were angled to address this critical issue?

Mind your language

There is a lot of talk about the importance of words these days. The twenty-first century has become obsessed with the meaning of words. And increasingly, therefore, words have set up barriers or drawbridges between communities. Some of the most used words imported from the last century include *sexism, ageism* and *racism*. They are the great *isms* of the twentieth century. These words appeared as inhibitors to justice. The difficulty we face is that they have become terribly politicised. As a society these words can do little to change our attitudes. And attitudes can kill.

Even more distressing is the fact that the very politicisation of such important words has set up negative reactions in the minds of many people who have become impatient with 'political correctness'. Women, elderly and disabled people are still disadvantaged in society. The fact that racism still exists over 30 years after it was outlawed, with the current leader of the Commission for Racial Equality, Trevor Phillips, being more vocal than ever on the issue of race, is an indication that something else is needed. Clearly, despite our shared diversity, our social interactions are as complex and fraught as ever.

In the eighteenth century the great slogan of the Abolitionist Movement raised a crucial question for slave-holders: 'Am I not a Man and a Brother?' Personhood and what it means to be human is the urgent question of the day.

The transition from segregated cultures to multiculturalism is now so marked that the time may have come to dismiss 'racism' altogether as a useful social indicator. Race is even waning as a political category. Anti-racism by definition is polemic and reactionary. It is even harder than fighting injustice or poverty. These can be measured: give money to build a school, sponsor a child, build a hospital and see the photographs. Anti-racism cannot produce anything – it is simply a policy of social restraint. In fact the more this issue is pushed, the more it is evoking negative reactions. Politicians cannot afford to say so, they can only shift the political goalposts; in the near future the Commission for Racial Equality is expected to reformulate into a combination of diversity and human rights issues.

Respect is central to the Christian worldview, for it touches all aspects of human encounters from the womb to the grave. Respect for life begins in the womb. It is not just anti-abortion but thoroughly pro-life in its commitment to human relationships. Christians grieve for the brutalised unborn in prosperous Western clinics as we grieve the death of some 20,000 children who die each day from poverty-related illnesses.

We are called not merely to react to evil, but to bring something more fundamental to the debate about diversity and society's well-being. It is to talk about and talk up 'respect' of persons. It is the heart of the message being conveyed by Christian ministries such as the Jubilee Centre and its focus on Relationship Foundation. It is a conviction rooted in our belief that people are

fundamentally made in God's image. Men and women,
black or white, young and old – all bear his image and
are therefore due reverential respect.

APPLICATION

1. As Christians we believe that Christ has made us one
   in him (Galatians 3:28), but do we believe that all
   humanity bears his image (Genesis 1:27)? We might
   need to repent before we can act.
2. When we look in the mirror, do we see the image of
   God reflected back? What do others see when they
   look at us?

Conclusion: Added Value

In the middle of the day a despised woman strode up to the well under the watch of the inhospitably blazing sun. As she approached through the haze of the midday heat she saw a stranger – a man whom she knew at a glance was very different from her. He was Jewish and she a Samaritan.

She had no plans to say much. It was bad enough that he was sat exactly where she wanted to draw water, but social discourse with a man in broad daylight was the last thing her reputation needed. But he started the conversation. It was a totally innocent question: he wanted a drink of water. No need for interpretation. Everyone needed water to drink. But it was a curious question for the average Jew, who would rather die of thirst than ask a Samaritan woman for a drink!

It was the most natural conversation. It moved from water to religion, personal transformation and then a whole village caught up in the overflow of this conversation by the well.

I hope that for Christians who struggle to start the conversation, and for churches who are programmed out, our focus on values will provide an easy way into the conversations of our culture. The object of the exercise is not to address these themes in isolation. Our aim is to examine the missing values in our society and to provide a Christian response.

As I said in the opening chapter, using values as a framework to engage with our society is not an attempt to replace classical forms of evangelism, preaching or Christian witness.

We have looked at the biblical trio of faith, hope and love, as Christian virtues with a secular interface of trust, hope and respect. The list of lost values is not exhausted by our focus on these three. Future themes will include *responsibility*, *rights* and *tolerance*. Increasingly we hope to draw on the growing thinking on these key themes of our day. We want to enable Christians to become involved in the dialogue, and engage decision-makers through public debate. And we will encourage this through preaching and small group resources, as well as an active website, as highlighted on the Resources page. Far from becoming an imposing programme for the local church, this Values engagement aims to provide creative ideas for individuals and local churches to use in their own communities and offer Christian perspectives on these important themes.

Our website www.valueseauk.org will furnish you with examples of good models and resources as the dialogue continues.

Finally, our focus on values is not a detached academic exercise. All around us there is a whirlwind of inquiry gathering pace. Much of the old order is disappearing and with it the old certainties. The implosion of our society has all the force of a tower block coming down. And it is as magnificent as it is destructive. We are enthralled by our new freedoms but in the absence of so many of the old absolutes we remain anxious about the future of our brave free world.

In our culture's nervous reluctance to talk about the old absolutes of truth or God, it appears that the quest for values is as good as it gets. And our nervousness is working itself out in the destabilising patterns of our relationships: broken homes, dysfunctional behaviour, crime and unprecedented levels of mistrust in public life.

Our search for Values is, I believe, part of the new thing that we have not created but which is quietly re-creating us. In this search we must inevitably ask the hidden questions again: Who are we? Where did we come from and where are we all going? And more than that: Who will help us get there?

The wind is gathering pace and these questions are a part of a wider canvas on which God, I believe, is making his own quiet mark on the pavements of our society as well as in the quiet corners of his Church. Falling numbers and a loss of morale overwhelm many. But that is not the whole story. There are many of us who believe that God still has the Church and society at heart and that his main agenda is the renewal of a failing Church and the transformation of a loved society. Our focus on values is therefore a small part of a movement for change that unites believing Christians to see positive change in our culture.

As the woman left her home that day in the silence of the siesta, she had no idea just how much that walk would change her life, reputation and relationship with those around her. Our hope and prayer is that as Christians feel increasingly empowered to strike up conversations, and our friends find the courage to listen, we too could become a part of the same story of changed lives and transformed communities.

Resources

Evangelical Alliance

The Evangelical Alliance represents over 1 million evangelical Christians in the UK. It aims to provide a voice, resources and network functions for its members and seeks to be at the heart of a movement for change in society. – http://www.eauk.org

Micah Challenge

The Micah Challenge is a global Christian campaign that challenges society to deepen its engagement with the poor, and challenges leaders to achieve the Millennium Development Goals – that is, to halve absolute global poverty by 2015. – http://www.micahchallenge.org

London Institute of Contemporary Christianity

LICC works to equip Christians to engage biblically and relevantly with the issues they face, including work, capitalism, youth culture, media, gender and communication – 'helping you to make a difference, where you are'. – http://www.licc.org.uk

The Jubilee Centre

The Jubilee Centre is a Christian think-tank seeking to research, disseminate and apply a biblical vision for society. Its work has spawned a wide range of organisations working to enhance interpersonal relationships, provide financial advice, and campaign on a broad spectrum of ethical/moral issues. –
http://www.jubilee-centre.org

CARE

CARE is a Christian charity involved in caring, campaigning and communicating across the UK. CARE is committed to being part of the answer in a society which so often asks 'who cares?' through a network of volunteers and activists, most of whom are supported by their Church. – http://www.care.org.uk

Ridley Hall Foundation

The Ridley Hall Foundation is an initiative relating Christian faith to the world of business. It is concerned with Faith in Business in a twofold way: affirming the role of business, as a legitimate, God-given part of human endeavour and exploring the operation of Christian faith in business. –
http://www.fibq.org/ridley-1

Lawyers Christian Fellowship

The LCF seeks to encourage and equip Christian lawyers to be effective in their lives and work. It aims to lead lawyers to a personal commitment to Jesus Christ and promote Christian principles in our laws and legal systems. – http://www.lawcf.org/

Association of Christian Teachers

ACT is a non-denominational membership organisation which aims to provide professional and spiritual support to all Christians engaged in pre-school, primary, special, secondary and college education in England. – http://www.christian-teachers.org.uk

Christian Medical Fellowship

CMF seeks to impact the medical world through promoting fellowship, ethics, evangelism, student support, missionary support and publishing relevant literature for its members. – http://www.cmf.org.uk

UCCF

The CU movement's aim is to encourage the growth of witnessing communities of Christian students within the colleges and universities of the UK. – http://www.uccf.org.uk

Notes

1 David Attwood, *Changing Values* (Carlisle: Paternoster, 1998) p. 11.
2 David Cook, *Our National Life* (London: Monarch, 1998) p. 29.
3 Anna Robbins, 'Ethical Models for the Twilight Zone of Church and Culture', in David Hilborn (ed.), *Movement for Change* (Carlisle: Paternoster, 2004) p. 91.
4 Jürgen Moltmann, *God For a Secular Society* (London: SCM Press, 1999), p. 210.
5 Jonathan Sacks, *The Politics of Hope* (London: Vintage, 2000) p. 37.
6 See the resources page for more detailed information.
7 Walter Brueggemann (ed.), *Hope for the World* (Louisville: Westminster John Knox Press, 2001) p. 16.
8 Pete Lowman, *A Long Way East of Eden* (Carlisle: Paternoster, 2002) p. viii.
9 Pete Lowman, *A Long Way East of Eden*, p. vii.
10 Alister McGrath, *Christian Theology – An Introduction* (London: Blackwell, 1997) p. 550.
10 Walter Brueggemann (ed.), *Hope for the World*, p. 78.
11 Walter Bruggemann (ed.), *Hope for the World*, p. 78.
12 Jürgen Moltmann, *Theology of Hope* (Norwich: SCM Press, 2002) p. 7.
13 Richard Bauckham and Trevor Hart, *Hope Against Hope* (London: DLT, 1999) p. 54.
14 'A Knock at Midnight', published in *Strength to Love*, 1963.

[15] The Micah Challenge is becoming a global Christian response that encourages and challenges governments to fulfil their commitment to halve world poverty by the year 2015 through the Millennium Development Goals.

[16] W. Mundle in Colin Brown (ed.), *Dictionary of New Testament Theology* (Carlisle: Paternoster, 1992) p. 264.